INTERFACT ™

THE BOOK AND DISK THAT WORK TOGETHER

NCIENT GREECE

CHANHASSEN, MINNESOTA · LONDON

Book and disk by
act-two Ltd

Published by Two-Can Publishing,
18705 Lake Drive East, Chanhassen, MN 55317
1-800-328-3895
www.two-canpublishing.com

ISBN: 1-58728-455-3

2 4 6 8 10 9 7 5 3

Photographic Credits: Front cover AKG Photo
Ancient Art and Architecture Collection: p13 r, p14,p15 b, p20, p23 t
Bridgeman Art Library: p26 r, p27 b; ET Archive: p17, p34 l; Werner Forman: pp10-11
Micheal Holford: p13 t,c, p15 t, p19, p23 b, p24 t, p26 l, p27 t, p28, p34 tr, p46, p47;
Toby Maudsley: pp24-25 b; Zefa: p34 br
Illustration Credits: Mike Allport: pp8-27, p47, p48; Maxine Hamil: pp29-33

Printed in Hong Kong by Wing King Tong

INTERFACT

THE BOOK AND DISK ⟶ THAT WORK TOGETHER

INTERFACT will have you hooked in minutes –
and that's a fact!

● The disk is full of interactive
activities, puzzles, quizzes, and games
that are fun to do
and packed with
interesting facts.

Put your knowledge
of the ancient Greeks
to the test in a
challenging quiz!

● Open the
book and discover
more fascinating
information
highlighted with
lots of full-color
illustrations and
photographs.

Read up all about
the peoples of
ancient Greece
and the cities
they lived in.

● To get the most out of **INTERFACT,**
use the book and disk together. Look for
the special signs called Disk Links
and Bookmarks. To find out more,
turn to page 43.

23

BOOKMARK

DISK LINK
Do you need
advice about
life in ancient
Greece? Then
ask AT THE ORACLE.

Once you've launched
INTERFACT, you'll never
look back.

LOAD UP!
Go to **page 40** to find out how to load
your disk and click into action.

What's on the disk

HELP SCREEN

Learn how to use the disk in no time at all.

These are the controls the Help Screen will tell you how to use:
- arrow keys
- text boxes
- "hot" words

THE CITY ON THE HILL

Visit the ancient city of Athens!

Spend some time at the Acropolis. You'll discover the Parthenon, and you may even meet a god or two! Then, visit the agora to find out all about the ancient Greek way of life.

PAST TIMES

Let Plato and Aristotle take you on an exciting journey through time!

These great thinkers will give you the lowdown on Greece – from the early days to modern times. Learn how past events have helped to shape our world.

AT THE ORACLE

Are you full of questions about the ancient Greeks?

Then why not ask the Pythia? This famous priestess has all the answers you'll ever need. Visit the oracle at Delphi and pop some questions.

THE WRITE STUFF

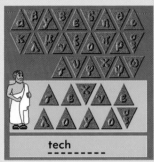

Take a good look at the letters of the Greek alphabet.

You'll find that Aristotle has what it takes to guide you through the Greek language. He has an epic story to tell – and he'll give you a few pointers on English as well!

ANCIENT ODYSSEY

You're going to guide Odysseus home to Ithaca, where his wife, Penelope, is waiting for him. To do this, you'll have to think like a true hero as you face some tough decisions. It's all up to you!

Go on an interactive adventure in ancient Greece!

Are you feeling heroic? Then get ready to take part in this exciting adventure game! You'll meet Odysseus, an ancient hero, and together you'll go on a journey to remember!

OLYMPIC CHALLENGE

When did the ancient Greek civilization begin?
- Around 3000 BC
- Around 2000 BC
- Around 1000 BC

Are you a champion when it comes to ancient Greece?

Take part in this challenging quiz. Every correct answer will help you to compete in the javelin event. So, the more you know, the farther you'll throw!

THE STATE OF THINGS

You've clicked on Macedonia, a country to the north of Greece.

Try putting the city-states in their place!

The Greek territories are in quite a state. If you can put things in order, you'll learn about who were friends and who were enemies in the ancient Greek world.

What's in the book

*All words in the text that appear in **bold** can be found in the glossary*

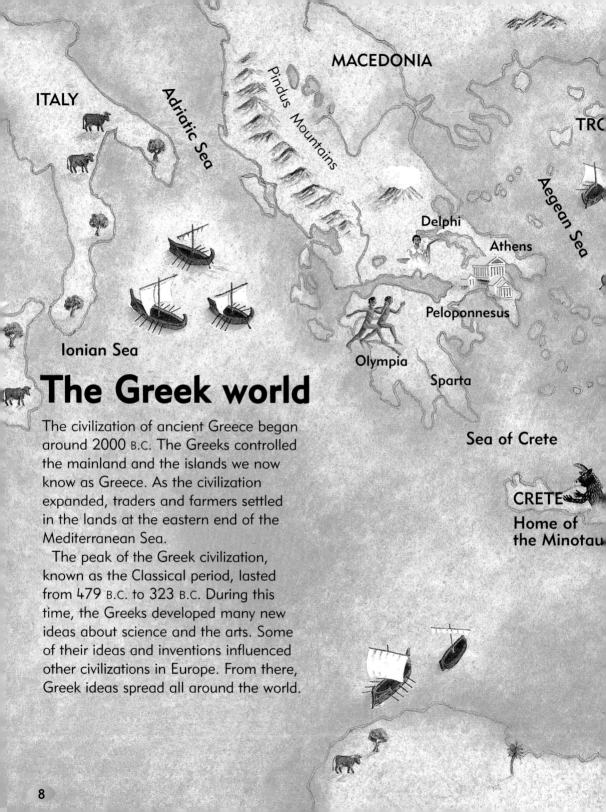

ITALY

Adriatic Sea

Pindus Mountains

MACEDONIA

TRO

Aegean Sea

Delphi

Athens

Peloponnesus

Ionian Sea

Olympia

Sparta

Sea of Crete

CRETE
Home of
the Minotau

The Greek world

The civilization of ancient Greece began
around 2000 B.C. The Greeks controlled
the mainland and the islands we now
know as Greece. As the civilization
expanded, traders and farmers settled
in the lands at the eastern end of the
Mediterranean Sea.

The peak of the Greek civilization,
known as the Classical period, lasted
from 479 B.C. to 323 B.C. During this
time, the Greeks developed many new
ideas about science and the arts. Some
of their ideas and inventions influenced
other civilizations in Europe. From there,
Greek ideas spread all around the world.

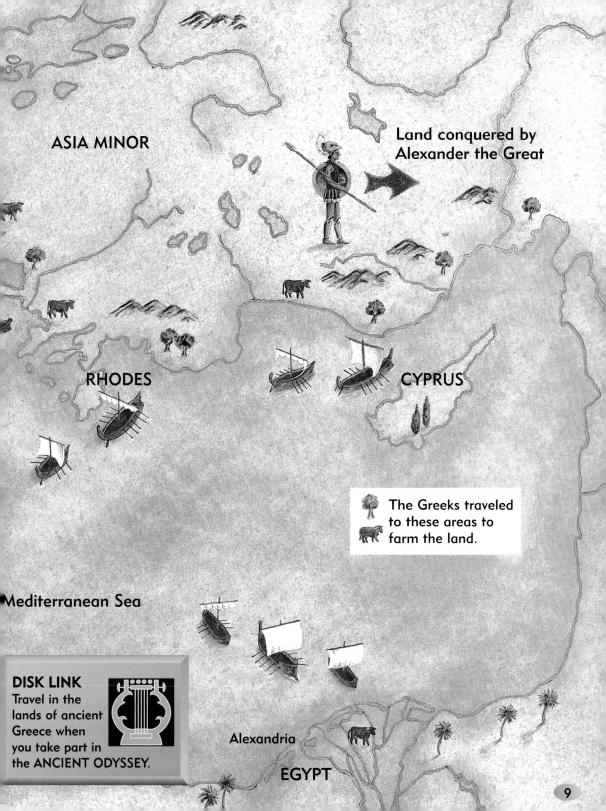

ASIA MINOR

Land conquered by
Alexander the Great

RHODES

CYPRUS

The Greeks traveled
to these areas to
farm the land.

Mediterranean Sea

DISK LINK
Travel in the
lands of ancient
Greece when
you take part in
the ANCIENT ODYSSEY.

Alexandria

EGYPT

Land and climate

Mainland Greece and the nearby islands are hot and dry, with high mountains and steep-sided valleys. The mainland is surrounded almost entirely by water. It was once covered in forest, but by the Classical period many trees had been cut down. The scarce farmland was mainly near the coast or in sheltered valleys.

The most important crops were wheat, barley, grapes, and olives. The Greeks were skilled sailors and clever traders, and they imported a lot of their food. There were few good roads, and most journeys had to be made on foot. Some of the village communities were very isolated.

▼ Because traveling overland was so difficult, the Greeks often traveled by sea. They found their way by staying close to the coasts. The sea was often stormy, and pirates sometimes attacked.

▶ This picture shows olive trees growing on a dry, rocky hillside.

DISK LINK
Do you want to know more about the land? Then take a look at **THE STATE OF THINGS.**

The city-states

Greece was not always a united country as it is today. It was once made up of separate city-states. Each city-state was based around one city and included the surrounding farms and villages.

Athens was one of the largest and most powerful city-states. At the height of the Classical period, more than 250,000 people lived in the city and the surrounding countryside. Artists, philosophers, and politicians from Athens were famous throughout Greece.

▼ This is the ancient city of Athens. On a hill called the **Acropolis** stood the Parthenon, the main temple of the city. In the center of town was the busy **agora**, where markets took place.

DISK LINK
See all the sights when you visit the ancient city of Athens in THE CITY ON THE HILL.

Athens vs. Sparta

Sparta was Athens' main rival. These two cities fought many wars as they both tried to gain control of the whole of Greece. Sparta was famed for the strength of its army. In 431 B.C., the rivalry between the two cities led to the Peloponnesian War. After 27 years of fighting, Sparta won the war.

▲ This vase painting shows Greek soldiers in battle.

▲ Ancient Greek soldiers used weapons and armor made from iron or bronze.

Citizens and slaves

In ancient Greece, some groups of people had more rights than others. **Citizens** were the most important group of people, and they had the most rights. They could own property and take part in politics. Only adult men were allowed to be citizens in ancient Greece.

 Slaves were the property of their owners, and they had no rights at all. Many slaves lived in miserable conditions. But some slaves were paid for the work that they did and if they saved enough money, they could buy their freedom.

▲ These are ancient Greek coins.

▼ Soldiers often watched over slaves as they worked.

DISK LINK
Read these pages very carefully! You might find some clues that will help you in the OLYMPIC CHALLENGE!

▲ This vase painting shows women collecting water. Women didn't have the same rights as men in ancient Greece.

Government

In many of the city-states in ancient Greece, the government was run as a **democracy**. All of the decisions about the city-state were made by councils of citizens. Other city-states, however, were ruled by rich and powerful landowners.

In Athens, all citizens could vote to decide on issues such as the type of taxes to be paid and whether or not to go to war. All citizens could take part in politics and legal affairs. Some citizens were paid a full day's wages to attend the government assemblies.

▲ Discs such as these were used to vote in courts of law. Hollow discs stood for "guilty," and solid discs stood for "not guilty."

▲ Citizens could vote against a politician by writing his name on a pottery fragment called an **ostrakon**.

Philosophy and science

The ancient Greeks were curious about themselves and the world around them. They made many important advances in science, learning, and the arts. Great thinkers were known as **philosophers**, no matter what subject they studied. The word philosopher comes from the Greek words for "lover of wisdom." Philosophers tried to find out how the universe worked and how people should best live their lives.

Many Greek discoveries provide the foundations of our knowledge and beliefs.

The Greeks studied the stars and learned that the earth floats freely in space and rotates on an imaginary line called an axis. They also correctly predicted eclipses of the sun. But sometimes the Greeks were wrong. A scholar named Ptolemy thought that the earth was the center of the universe.

Few of the Greeks' ideas were used for solving practical problems. For example, they did not use their metal-working techniques to make tools that would increase their knowledge of science.

Famous philosophers

● **Socrates** (about 470 - 399 B.C.)
Socrates was one of the first great philosophers of Classical Greece. He questioned many of the beliefs of the time.

● **Hippocrates** (about 460 - 380 B.C.)
Hippocrates was alive at the same time as Socrates. He practiced scientific medicine and studied the human body.

● **Plato** (about 427 - 347 B.C.)
Plato founded a school in Athens called The Academy, where he taught Aristotle.

● **Aristotle** (384 - 322 B.C.)
Aristotle examined things in nature and developed a way of thinking called **logic**.

▲ A bust of Socrates

◄ The philosopher Eratosthenes used geometry to calculate the circumference of the earth. He compared the angle of the sun's shadow at Alexandria and Syene, in Egypt. Knowing the distance between the two cities and knowing that the earth was round, he was able to make a fairly accurate calculation. It was off by no more than 4,140 miles (6,624 km).

DISK LINK
Would you like to meet some great thinkers? Then take a look at PAST TIMES.

Gods and goddesses

The Greeks worshiped many gods and goddesses that represented parts of human life or the natural world. The gods were thought to live on **Mount Olympus**, and there were many stories about them, in which they fought among one another or fell in love just like men and women.

The Greeks built many temples where priests or priestesses performed rituals in honor of the gods. Offerings of food and wine were made, and sometimes **sacrifices** were made during festivals.

The Greeks believed that the gods controlled events. So they looked to the gods for answers to their problems. Some problems were solved by a **soothsayer**, who studied the weather or the remains of animals for answers from the gods. Other problems required a visit to an **oracle**, where a priest or priestess passed on messages from the gods.

▼ **At the oracle in Delphi, a priestess called the Pythia went into a trance to receive messages from the gods.**

The Olympic Games

The ancient Greeks held games and festivals to honor the gods. The Olympic Games were held in Olympia in honor of Zeus every four years. They lasted for five days, and the events included boxing, wrestling, running, long-jump, discus throwing, javelin throwing, and chariot races. People came from all over Greece to compete in the games. All wars were postponed so that people could travel safely to see them.

Important gods

ZEUS was the king of the gods.
HERA was married to Zeus. She was the queen of the gods.
POSEIDON was the god of the sea.
DIONYSUS was the god of wine.
ARES was the god of war.
HERMES was the messenger of the gods.
APOLLO was the god of music and healing.

▲ Aphrodite, the goddess of love

◄ Athena, the goddess of wisdom, was born from the head of Zeus.

Theater and writing

The Greeks were among the first people to record their history as it happened. Before this, people had passed on history by word of mouth. Poetry was the earliest form of Greek literature. Many of the poems told stories about heroes and gods. Homer, an ancient storyteller, is traditionally considered the composer of two **epic** poems, the *Iliad* and the *Odyssey*. These and many other examples of Greek literature have survived until today.

▲ The actors in comedies wore padded costumes to make them look funny.

Drama

Drama developed from songs and dances that honored the gods. Plays were an important part of religious festivals, and many of the theaters were built next to temples. There were two types of plays: tragedies and comedies. Tragedies were sad tales about gods, heroes, and legendary people. Comedies made fun of politics, religion, and important people.

▶ Greek actors always wore masks that showed different moods and expressions. The masks had wide mouths so that the actors' voices could be heard.

DISK LINK
Is Greek a lot like English? You'll find out if you've got **THE WRITE STUFF!**

At home

In ancient Greece, ordinary people lived in simple houses made from mud bricks. It was so easy to dig through the walls that burglars were known as wall-diggers! Each house was arranged around a courtyard with an altar in the middle. The living rooms were on the ground floor, with bedrooms above.

Men and women often had separate living areas and spent most of their time apart. Open fires burned in the kitchen, and smoke escaped through a hole in the roof.

▼ **This is the inside of a typical ancient Greek house.**

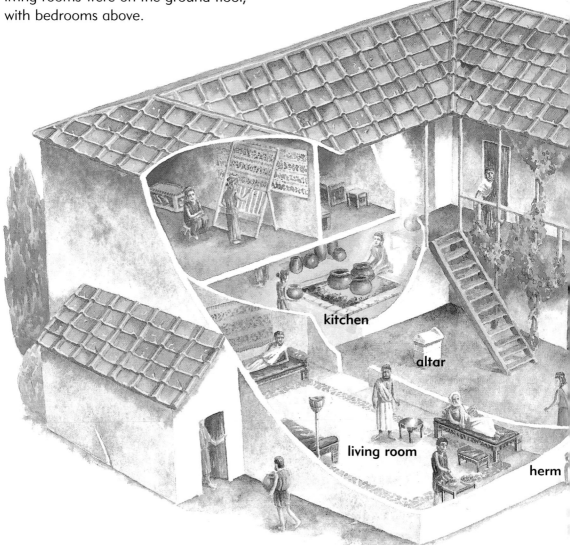

kitchen

altar

living room

herm

Clothes

Men in ancient Greece wore tunics made from wool or linen. Over this, they wore a square piece of material called a **chiton**, fastened at the shoulders and belted at the waist. In colder weather, men draped a cloak called a **himation** around them. In Classical times, it was very fashionable for men to have beards.

Women wore a long tunic called a **peplos**. Wealthy people wore tunics made from decorated material, while slaves had plain tunics. Shoes were leather sandals or boots, but many people went barefoot.

▼ A gold necklace similar to the one worn by the woman in the vase painting below.

bathroom

ell

▶ This vase painting shows a woman getting ready for her wedding. She is wearing a peplos.

◀ Some houses had a statue of the god Hermes, called a herm, to guard the house.

Food

The ancient Greeks had a simple and healthful diet. They ate bread, cheese, fruit, vegetables, eggs, and meat. Many Greeks lived near the sea, so fish and seafood were popular. Olive oil was used for cooking, lighting, and cleaning.

The main meal was in the evening, and the Greeks often held big dinner parties. They sat on couches, eating several courses and drinking lots of wine. After the meal, there was entertainment for the men at a **symposium**, or drinking party.

DISK LINK
Keep your eyes peeled for information to help you in the OLYMPIC CHALLENGE!

▲ This vase painting shows a messenger of the gods bringing a gift of grain.

▼ These are some examples of fruits that the ancient Greeks liked to eat.

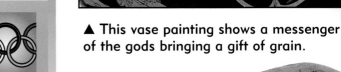

pomegranates

figs

olives

dried dates

fresh da

Greek sweetmeats

Between courses at a dinner party, the Greeks ate sweetmeats – small snacks made from dates, figs, nuts, sesame seeds, and honey. Here are some for you to make.

Put 1 cup (100 g) of sesame seeds into a saucepan with 4 large tablespoons of honey. Ask an adult to help you simmer the mixture over a low heat for 10-20 minutes, until it is a rich, golden color. You can tell if it is ready by dropping a spoonful onto a wet plate, letting it cool, then working it into a ball. If it keeps its shape, it is ready. Take the pan off the heat and stir the mixture every few minutes until it is almost cold. Wet your hands with cold water and roll spoonfuls of the mixture into 20 to 25 little balls. Wrap each sweetmeat in waxed paper.

grapes

Arts and crafts

The Greeks thought that there was a perfect shape for every object, whether it was a simple clay pot or a huge temple. They used mathematics to try to make their art as beautiful as possible.

▲ The Greeks made elegant pots covered in patterns and paintings. Most of the pots were used every day, for storing water, oil, or wine. Some of the most beautiful pots were buried with the dead.

◄ This statue is made from stone. The Greeks were skilled sculptors, and they made many statues from stone or bronze. The statues were detailed and lifelike, with expressive faces and clothes that looked real. Many of them were painted, but they have lost their color over time.

This is the Parthenon, in Athens. It is one of the finest examples of ancient Greek architecture that is still standing today. It was made from carved blocks of cream-colored marble, held together with wooden pegs and metal clamps. The rows of columns are typical of ancient Greek buildings. This Classical style has been copied all over the world.

Bronze statues

Bronze statues were made using the lost wax method.

▼ When the clay was finally removed, a bronze statue was revealed.

Firstly, a clay model was made. Wooden pegs were used to hold it together. Then, the model was covered with a thin layer of wax. The details of the statue's face and clothes were sculpted onto the wax.

The model was then covered with clay and heated so that the wax melted and ran out. Molten bronze was poured in between the clay layers.

Language and learning

In ancient Greece, most children went to school. Boys went to school from the age of seven until they were 15. Boys learned reading, writing, and math, as well as music, poetry, and sports. Some girls learned reading, writing, gymnastics, and music. Girls were also taught the skills that they would need to run a household.

In Sparta, boys were taught to be tough to prepare them for their life as soldiers. At the age of seven, they went to a strict school where they learned how to fight and use weapons. They often went hungry and had to sleep on the ground, and sometimes they were beaten.

▶ This ancient terra cotta doll has jointed arms and legs.

◀ This is an ancient baby bottle.

The Greek alphabet

Some Greek letters are similar to those we use today. You may have heard some of their names before. Can you guess where our word *alphabet* comes from?

Greek letter	Name	English sound	Greek letter	Name	English sound	Greek letter	Name	English sound	Greek letter	Name	English sound
A α	alpha	a	H η	eta	ey	N ν	nu	n	T τ	tau	t
B β	beta	b	Θ θ	theta	th	Ξ ξ	xi	ks	Y υ	upsilon	u
Γ γ	gamma	g	I ι	iota	i	O o	omicron	o	Φ φ	phi	ph
Δ δ	delta	d	K κ	kappa	k	Π π	pi	p	X χ	chi	ch
E ε	epsilon	e	Λ λ	lambda	l	P ρ	rho	r	Ψ ψ	psi	ps
Z ζ	zeta	z	M μ	mu	m	Σ σ,ς	sigma	s	Ω ω	omega	oh

The legend of the Minotaur

The ancient Greeks told **myths** about their gods and about the world around them.
Myths often included real events from Greek history. This myth is about an
early civilization on the island of Crete, long before Athens was a powerful city-state.
It tells the story of Theseus, a heroic young man who overcame the Minotaur,
a terrifying beast that was half man and half bull.

Athenians were afraid of the island of Crete and trembled at the mention of it. Every nine years, King Minos of Crete demanded a terrible tribute from the Athenians. Seven young men and seven young women were taken from Athens to be fed to the fearsome Minotaur. King Minos would send a ship with black sails to Athens when the tribute was due. A huge crowd would gather at the harbor, weeping and wailing as their beautiful young people sailed away toward Crete.

When the prisoners arrived in Crete, they were given fine clothes and made guests of honor at a huge banquet. They were offered the most delicious food available, but they could hardly eat. Afterward, they were shut in a luxurious room, but few of them could sleep.

The next day, they were taken to a set of huge wooden doors carved with pictures of galloping bulls. From behind the doors came loud bellowing and stamping. The prisoners were very afraid.

Then a guard opened the doors and pushed a prisoner through. The small crowd of prisoners, guards, and priestesses outside heard a blood-curdling scream. A priestess pointed at the next prisoner to be sent through. This went on until all the prisoners had met their fate. Afterward, the Athenians rested easy for nine years, until it was time to make another tribute.

One year when the dreaded tribute was due, a young man named Theseus was among the prisoners. Unlike all the other prisoners, he sat dry-eyed on the ship. His laughter and happy chatter cheered the other prisoners as they prepared for the banquet. At the banquet, Theseus sat next to King Minos' daughter, Ariadne, who was charmed by his courage and his handsome looks.

Ariadne told Theseus that behind the doors there was an elaborate maze. The paths twisted and turned, confusing the eye and the mind. No one who had entered the maze had ever returned.

The Minotaur lived at the very heart of the maze. He knew all the twists, turns, and blind alleys. Within moments, the Minotaur could find anyone who stumbled into the maze.

Ariadne was determined to help Theseus. After the banquet, she crept into the sleeping chamber and called softly to him. Ariadne handed him a sword. Then she led the way to the great carved wooden doors of the maze.

"I will wait here for you," she said and handed Theseus a ball of thread.

"What is this for?" Theseus said, puzzled.

"As you walk through the maze, unwind

this thread behind you. If you succeed, you can follow the thread back. The Minotaur will be asleep, so creep silently through the passages until you reach his lair. With surprise on your side, you may beat him," Ariadne said.

Theseus took the thread from Ariadne and pushed open the great door. He stepped inside and closed the door, trapping the end of the thread in it. Then, holding his sword in front of him, Theseus headed into the maze.

Theseus could hear the Minotaur snoring and headed toward the noise. But a few minutes later, he could no longer hear the snores. The path had doubled back, and he was farther away from the center than when he had started. Theseus picked up the thread and followed it back to the last place where he had chosen a path.

"If I take the path that seems to lead toward the Minotaur, I end up farther away," he said to himself. "But perhaps if I choose the path that seems to lead away, I will get closer to him."

Theseus crept quietly along and soon

found himself stumbling into the mouth of a dark cave. From inside, he heard a huge roar, followed by the sound of heavy footsteps. The Minotaur had awakened!

Theseus gasped and dropped his sword. The Minotaur was even more terrifying than he had imagined. It had the body of a huge man and the head of an angry bull. Just as the Minotaur leapt forward to grab him, Theseus picked up his sword and struck the Minotaur a terrible blow on the leg.

The Minotaur was in agony. He was not used to people fighting back – his victims were usually prisoners who did not resist. Theseus struck once more with his sword. The Minotaur lay dead at his feet!

Picking up the end of the thread, brave Theseus retraced his steps through the maze. Ariadne waited for him at the outer doors.

Theseus was proclaimed a hero by the people of Athens. They were overjoyed that Athens no longer had to pay such a terrible tribute to King Minos of Crete.

How we know

How do we know so much about the Greeks when they lived so long ago?

Evidence from the ground

The Greeks built many buildings and made many beautiful objects. Some were buried, and archaeologists have been able to dig them up to learn from them. Pictures on pottery, for example, tell us about the way people looked.

▲ The painting on this plate shows two Greek heroes fighting over the body of a soldier.

Evidence from around us

Greek buildings that remain standing today give us evidence of how the ancient Greeks lived. And some Greek words have become part of other European languages, especially words connected with science, like *psychology* and *astronomy*.

▲ This picture is from Roman times. It shows Alexander the Great, a famous Greek military leader, going into battle against the Persian Empire.

Evidence from books

The ancient Greeks were one of the first groups of people to keep written records. They wrote down all sorts of things, from history and philosophy, to lists of goods in stores. Many of these have survived until today. They give us important clues about the ancient Greek way of life.

▲ Theseus' temple still stands in Athens.

Glossary

Acropolis
The hill within the boundary of a city-state that was used for defense. *Acropolis* means "high city."

agora
An open area in the center of ancient Greek cities where markets took place.

chiton
A garment Greek men wore fastened at the shoulders and belted around the waist.

citizen
In ancient Greece, a citizen was a man who had the right to own property and take part in politics and the law.

democracy
A political system where citizens can vote for their leaders and can influence decisions about the way their city or country is run.

epic
A long, traditional poem that tells a story about heroes or gods.

himation
A type of cloak worn by Greek men.

logic
A method of thinking a problem through carefully to find a solution.

Mount Olympus
The mountain in Greece where the gods were thought to live.

myths
Traditional stories about gods or heroes.

oracle
A holy place where priests and priestesses asked the gods for advice.

ostrakon
A pottery fragment that citizens wrote on to vote against a politician.

peplos
A long tunic worn by women in ancient Greece.

philosopher
A person who studies the world. This word comes from the Greek words for "lover of wisdom."

sacrifice
An offering, usually of an animal, made to the gods, asking them to bring good fortune to people.

slave
A worker who was owned by a citizen and had no rights at all.

soothsayer
A person who could predict the future and tell fortunes.

symposium
A drinking party, attended by Greek men, where entertainment took place.

Lab pages

Photocopy these sheets and use them to make your own notes.

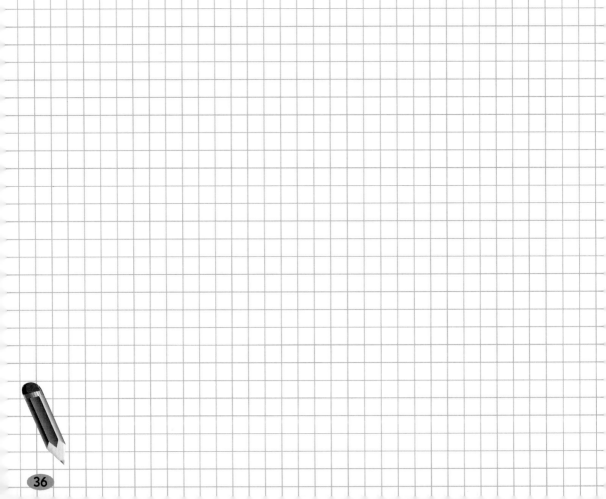

36

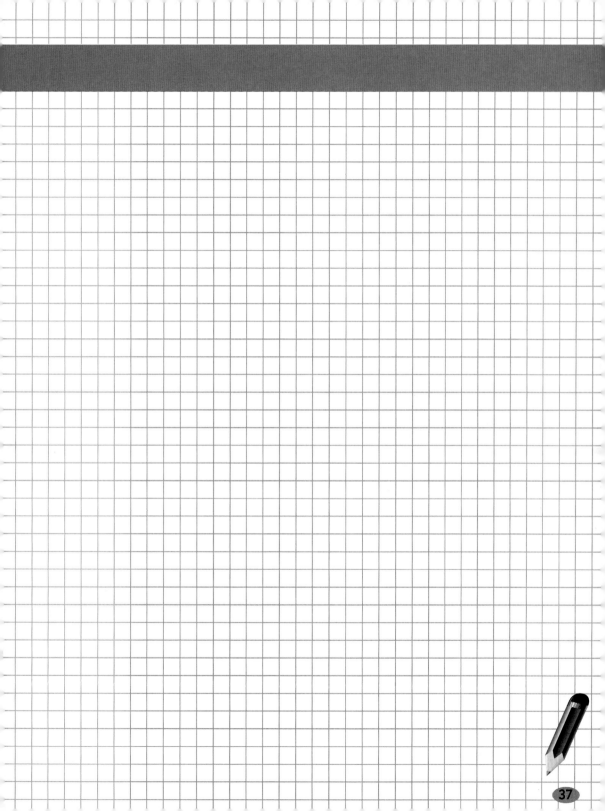

Lab pages

Photocopy these sheets and use them to make your own notes.

Loading your INTERFACT disk

INTERFACT is available on floppy disk and CD-ROM for both PCs with Windows and Apple Macs. Make sure you follow the correct instructions for the disk you have chosen and your type of computer. Before you begin, check the minimum specification (inside front cover).

CD-ROM INSTRUCTIONS

If you have a copy of INTERFACT on CD, you can run the program from the disk – you don't need to install it on your hard drive.

PC WITH WINDOWS 95

1. Put the disk in the CD drive
2. Open MY COMPUTER
3. Double click on the CD drive icon
4. Double click on the icon called GREECE

PC WITH WINDOWS 3.1 OR 3.11

1. Put the disk in the CD drive
2. Select RUN from the FILE menu in the PROGRAM MANAGER
3. Type **D:\GREECE** (Where D is the letter of your CD drive)
4. Press the RETURN key

APPLE MAC

1. Put the disk in the CD drive
2. Double click on the INTERFACT icon
3. Double click on the icon called GREECE

FLOPPY DISK INSTRUCTIONS

If you have a copy of INTERFACT on floppy disk you must install the program on to your computer's hard drive before you can run it.

PC WITH WINDOWS 95

To install INTERFACT:
1. Put the disk in the floppy drive
2. Select RUN from the START menu
3. Type **A:\INSTALL** (Where A is the letter of your floppy drive)
4. Click OK – unless you want to change the name of the INTERFACT directory

To run INTERFACT:
Once the program has installed, open the START menu and select PROGRAMS then select INTERFACT and click on the icon called GREECE

PC WITH WINDOWS 3.1 OR 3.11

To install INTERFACT:
1. Put the disk in the floppy drive
2. Select RUN from the FILE menu in the PROGRAM MANAGER
3. Type **A:\INSTALL** (Where A is the letter of your floppy drive)
4. Click OK – unless you want to change the name of the INTERFACT directory

To run INTERFACT:
Once the program has installed, open the INTERFACT group in the PROGRAM MANAGER and double click on the icon called GREECE

APPLE MAC

To install INTERFACT:
1. Put the disk in the floppy drive
2. Double click on the icon called INTERFACT INSTALLER
3. Click CONTINUE
4. Click INSTALL – unless you want to change the name of the INTERFACT folder

To run INTERFACT:
Once the program has installed, open the INTERFACT folder and double click on the icon called GREECE

How to use INTERFACT

INTERFACT is easy to use.
First see page 38 to find out how to load the
program. Then read these simple
instructions and dive in!

There are seven different features to explore. Use the controls on the right-hand side of the screen to select the one you want to play. You will see that the main area of the screen changes as you click on different features.

For example, this is what your screen will look like when you play AT THE ORACLE, where the Pythia will answer all your questions. Once you've selected a feature, click on the main screen to start playing.

What did the Greeks discover about maths and science?

Click on the Pythia for the answer.

Click here to select the feature you want to play.

Click on the arrow keys to scroll through the different features on the disk or find your way to the exit.

This is the text box, where instructions and directions appear. See page 4 to find out what's on the disk.

DISK LINKS

When you read the book, you'll come across Disk Links. These show you where to find activities on the disk that relate to the page you are reading. Use the arrow keys to find the icon on screen that matches the one in the Disk Link.

DISK LINK
Would you like to see the Acropolis? You can when you visit the CITY ON THE HILL!

BOOKMARKS

As you explore the features on the disk, you'll bump into Bookmarks. These show you where to look in the book for more information about the topic on screen. Just turn to the page of the book shown in the Bookmark.

LAB PAGES

On pages 36 – 37, you'll find note pages for you to photocopy. These are for making notes and recording any thoughts or ideas you may have about what you've read.

HOT DISK TIPS

● If you don't know how to use one of the on-screen controls, simply touch it with your cursor. An explanation will pop up in the text box!

● Any words that appear on screen in a different color and underlined are "hot." This means that you can touch them with the cursor for more information.

● Keep a close eye on the cursor. When it changes from an arrow to a hand, click your mouse and something will happen.

● After you have chosen the feature you want to play, remember to move the cursor from the icon to the main screen before clicking your mouse again.

Troubleshooting

If you have a problem with your INTERFACT disk, you should find the solution here. You can also e-mail for help at info@creativepub.com

COMMON PROBLEMS

Cannot load disk
There is not enough space available on your hard disk. To make more space available, delete old applications and programs you don't use until 6 MB of free space is available.

There is no sound (PCs only)
Your sound card is not SoundBlaster compatible. To make your settings SoundBlaster compatible, see your sound card manual for more information.

Disk will not run
There is not enough memory available. Quit all other applications and programs. If this does not work, increase your machine's RAM by adjusting the Virtual Memory (see right).

There is no sound
Your speakers or headphones are not connected to the CD-ROM drive. Ensure that your speakers or headphones are connected to the speaker outlet at the back of your computer.

Print-outs are not centered on the page or are partly cut off
Make sure that the page layout is set to "Landscape" in the Print dialog box.

There is no sound
Ensure that the volume control is turned up (on your external speakers and by using internal volume control).

Graphics freeze or text boxes appear blank (Windows 95 or 98 only)

Graphics card acceleration is too high. Right-click on MY COMPUTER. Click on SETTINGS (Windows 95) or PROPERTIES (Windows 98), then PERFORMANCE, then GRAPHICS. Reset the hardware acceleration slider to "None." Click OK. You may have to restart your computer.

Text does not fit into boxes or hot words do not work

The standard fonts on your computer have been moved or deleted. You must reinstall them. PC users need Arial. Macintosh users need Helvetica. Please see your computer manual for further information.

Your machine freezes

There is not enough memory available. Either quit other applications and programs or increase your machine's RAM by adjusting the Virtual Memory (see right).

Graphics do not load or are of poor quality

Not enough memory is available, or you have the wrong display setting. Either quit other applications and programs or make sure that your monitor control is set to 256 colors (Mac) or VGA (PC).

HOW TO...

Reset screen resolution in Windows 3.1 or 3.11:

In Program Manager, double-click on MAIN. Double-click on OPTIONS, then click on "Change system settings." Reset the screen resolution to 640 x 480, 256 Colors. Restart your computer after changing display settings.

Reset screen resolution in Windows 95 or 98:

Click on START at the bottom left of your screen, then click on SETTINGS, then CONTROL PANEL. Then double-click on DISPLAY. Click on the SETTINGS tab at the top. Reset the Desktop area (or Display area) to 640 x 480 pixels, then click APPLY. You may need to restart your computer after changing display settings.

Reset screen resolution for Macintosh:

Click on the Apple symbol at the top left of your screen to access APPLE MENU ITEMS. Select CONTROL PANELS, then MONITORS (or MONITORS AND SOUND). Set the resolution to 640 x 480.

Adjust the Virtual Memory on a PC with Windows 95 or 98:

Open MY COMPUTER, then click on CONTROL PANEL, then SYSTEMS. Select PERFORMANCE, click on VIRTUAL MEMORY, and set the preferred size to a higher value.

Adjust the Virtual Memory on a Macintosh:

If you have 16 MB of RAM or more, GREECE will run faster. Select the GREECE icon and go to GET INFO in the FILE folder. Set the preferred (or current) size to a higher value.

Index